D0842566

A Kid's Guide to
Origami™

Making Basic
ORIGAMI SHAPES
Step by Step

Michael G. LaFosse

The Rosen Publishing Group's
PowerKids Press™
New York

In memory of Molly Kahn, creator of the "Fox Box"

Published in 2002 by The Rosen Publishing Group, Inc.
29 East 21st Street, New York, NY 10010

First Edition

Book Design: Emily Muschinske
Project Editors: Jennifer Quasha, Jennifer Landau, and Jason Moring

Illustration Credits: Michael G. LaFosse
Photographs by Cindy Reiman, background image of paper crane on each page © CORBIS.

LaFosse, Michael G.
    Making origami shapes step by step / Michael G. LaFosse.—1st ed.
            p. cm. – (A kid's guide to origami)
Includes index.
    ISBN 0-8239-5872-8
  1. Origami—Juvenile literature. [1. Origami.] I. Title. II. Series.
    TT870 .L234 2002
    736'.982—dc21

                                                                        00-012006

Manufactured in the United States of America

Contents

What Is Origami?

Origami is paper folding. In Japanese, "ori" means fold and "kami" means paper. People in Japan have enjoyed this art for hundreds of years. Origami has become an important part of their culture. Today people all over the world practice origami.

Origami has a special language of **symbols**, just like music. No matter what country you are from, the language of origami is the same. Once you learn these symbols, you can read an origami book from any country, even from Japan!

Origami usually is folded from a single sheet of square paper, like all of the origami in this book. Most origami paper only has color on one side, but you do not need to buy special origami paper. You can make origami using old magazines, gift-wrapping paper, colorful notepapers, and even candy wrappers! Make sure that the paper is square and is the right size for your project. When you start a project, make sure the origami paper faces the way the instructions suggest. The key at the back of the book will help you make your origami projects.

Some wonderful origami projects use more than one sheet of paper. These projects are like puzzles. There are several of these designs in this book. By combining several simple folded shapes, you can **create** many kinds of decorations. As you try new ideas, you will **invent** your own origami puzzles and decorations.

Flower

The origami flower is a fun shape to know how to make. This simple flowering plant alone is a great gift. Together, a few flowers make pretty decorations for a springtime party. Create one for each of your guests, write their names on them, and place them on the table at their seats.

1

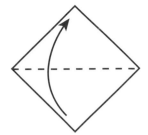

Use a square piece of colorful paper. If you are using origami paper, start with the white side up. Fold the bottom corner to the top corner to make a colored triangle.

2

Fold the two bottom corners of the triangle up, almost to the top. The paper should look like a tulip with three petals. Each point should be separate so that you can see all three of them.

3

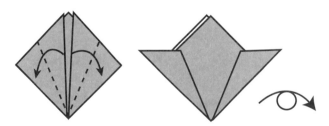

Fold out the folded edges, from the center, to align with folded edges on the bottom left and the bottom right of the diamond shape.

4

Fold into the center the bottom left and the bottom right edges of the diamond shape.

5

Fold up the bottom corner. Turn over the paper. This is the green plant part of this project.

6

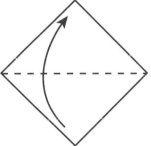

Use another square piece of paper. Fold the bottom corner to the top corner to make a triangle.

7

Fold up the two corners to make the petals of the flower.

8

Fit the bottom corner of the flower into the top of the plant.

Kite Star

Stars make wonderful decorations. You can make origami stars of all sizes and colors using different paper. Here is a creative way to use one simple shape, the kite, to build star shapes and patterns of folded paper. Once you learn how to make the shape, you will be able to invent new projects of your own. You will need four sheets of square paper to make the basic Kite Star. The four squares for each star must be the same size. You also will need clear tape.

1

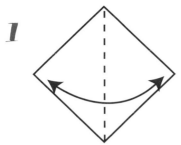

Begin with one piece of square paper. If you are using origami paper, start with the white side up. Fold the paper in half, from one corner to the other corner, to make a triangle shape. Now unfold.

2

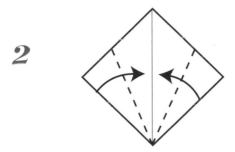

Fold the two bottom edges to the crease line at the middle of the paper.

3

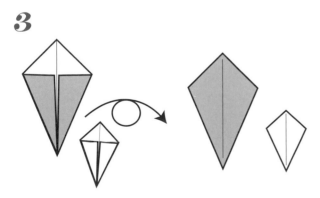

Now you have a kite shape! You can make big kites or small kites by using different sizes of square paper. Turn the kite over to see the display, or colorful, side of this origami shape. Now make three more. You need four same-size kites to make a Kite Star.

4

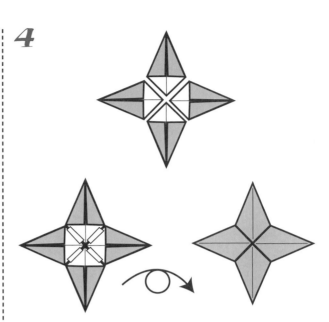

On the back, tape the four origami kites together to make one star. Turn over the taped papers to see your beautiful star.

5

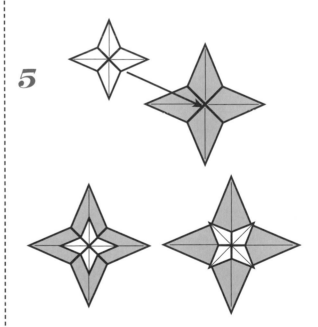

Repeat steps one through four using four smaller pieces of different colored paper. Turn the small star to match the same position as the larger star or rotate it so that the points are between the points of the larger star. Which way do you like it best?

Sunburst

Because this origami looks like the **brilliant** rays of the sun, we call it a Sunburst. This project is like the Kite Star. If you have made a Kite Star, you can make this Sunburst. Using three different colors of paper gives the best effect. You will need a total of 24 pieces of square paper for the Sunburst. You need eight squares for the large kites, eight squares (half the size of the paper for the large kites) for the small kites, and eight squares (the same size as the large kite papers) for the diamonds. You also will need clear tape.

1

To make a large kite, begin with one piece of square paper. If you are using origami paper, start with the white side up. Fold the paper in half, from one corner to the other corner, and then unfold.

2

Fold the two bottom edges to the crease line at the middle of the paper.

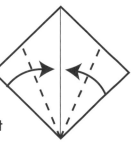

3

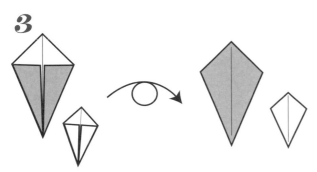

Now you have the kite shape! Make seven more kite shapes by repeating steps one and two seven more times. You can make big kites or small kites by using different sizes of square paper. Now make eight small kites the same way by using a different color of paper.

4

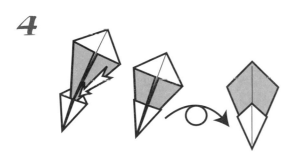

See how a large kite fits into a small kite? Turn the kites over to see the beautiful pattern. Put your eight large kites and your eight small kites together to build a Sunburst.

5

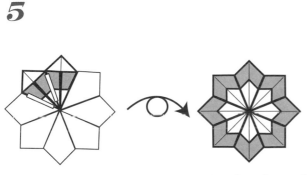

Tape the kites together on the back side and turn the paper over to see the beautiful design.

6

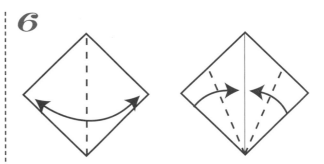

Use eight pieces of the same size square paper that you used to make your large kites. However, use a different color of paper. Fold the paper in half, from one corner to the other corner, and then unfold. Fold the bottom edges to the crease line in the middle of the paper. This is just like making a kite.

7

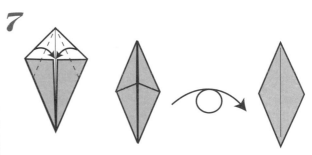

Fold the top, short edges of the kite to the middle to make a diamond shape. All four sides on this new diamond should be equal. Make seven more diamonds.

8

Push the eight diamonds into the top of the eight small kites.

Magic Square

Sometimes origami is called paper magic because a simple piece of paper is **transformed**, or changed, into something wonderful just by folding. Many magicians learn origami because it seems so "magical." Show this little piece of magic to your friends.

1

Begin with a square piece of paper that is a different color on each side. If you are using origami paper, start with the colored side up. Fold the paper in half, from the bottom edge to the top edge, and then unfold. Turn the square so that it looks like a diamond.

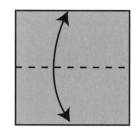

2

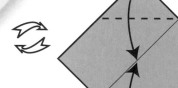

Fold the bottom and the top corners toward the center. Use the center line to guide your fold. Make sure the corner points meet in the middle of the paper.

3

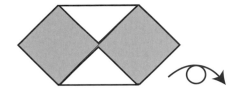

Both colors should show. This shape has six sides and is called a **hexagon**. "Hex" means six and "gon" means side. Take this hexagon, turn it over, and rotate.

6

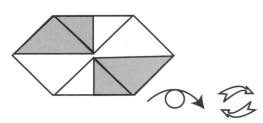

You have a hexagon shape again. See how different the shapes of the colors are now? Turn your paper over and rotate it.

4

 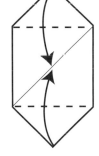 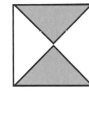

Like you did in step two, fold the bottom and the top corners to the center.

7

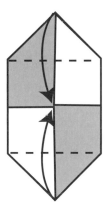

Fold the bottom and the top corners to the center.

5

 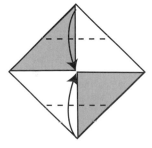

Position your folded paper in a diamond shape. Fold the bottom and top corners to the center like you did in step two.

8

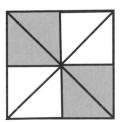

Now look at your square. The colored and white shapes changed from triangles to squares. Magic!

Star Frame

What is a frame? A frame surrounds a picture on all sides. Why do we make frames? Frames allow us to handle a picture without **damaging**, or hurting, it. Frames also can make the picture within it look better. Frames help people look at the picture and see it more clearly. Frames make pictures more special. You may want to use a frame sometime. Here is a way to make an origami frame from folded paper. You can use any type of square paper for this project. The bigger the picture is, the bigger the frame needs to be. The bigger the frame is, the bigger the paper needs to be.

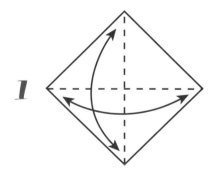

Begin with a square piece of paper. If you are using origami paper, start with the white side up. Fold the paper in half, from one corner to the other corner, to make a triangle. Open the paper and fold it in half the other way. See how the creases are crossed in the middle of the paper?

2

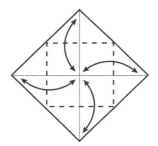

Neatly fold each corner of the square toward the center where the creases cross. Now unfold the corners. Look at the new creases you made. They make a square. Each new crease should cross one of the creases from step one.

3

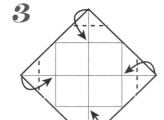 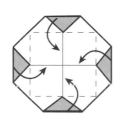

Fold each corner of the square to touch the closest line in front of it. Now fold the folded edges again. This will make a frame shape. The folds to do this are already in your paper. You made them in step two!

4

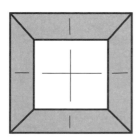

You can use this simple frame for a photograph or a picture. You can make a frame any size you want by using bigger or smaller paper. For an even prettier frame, follow the next steps to make a Star Frame.

5

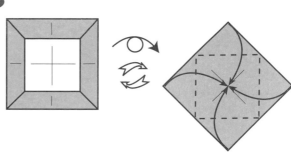

Turn your frame over and rotate it. Fold each of the four corners toward the center where the lines cross.

6

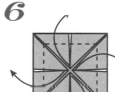 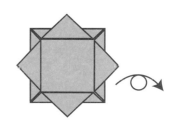

Take each corner from the middle of the paper and fold it out. You have made an eight-pointed star!

7

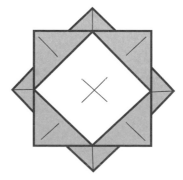

Turn over the paper. Now you have an eight-pointed Star Frame. You can put pictures in this frame and either keep it for yourself or give it as a gift.

Bookmark

A bookmark is an object that you put in your book to hold your place. This origami bookmark not only **marks**, or holds, your place, but it also tells you on which side of the page you were! It also stays in one place and will not fall out, like other bookmarks sometimes do.

You can make bookmarks for your friends, or even better, teach them how to make their own.

1

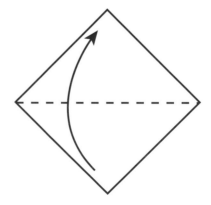

Use a square piece of paper 6 inches (15.2 cm) wide or less. If you are using origami paper, begin with the white side up. Fold the bottom corner to the top corner to make a triangle.

2

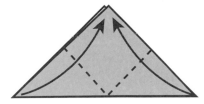

Making clean creases, fold the two bottom corners to the top.

3

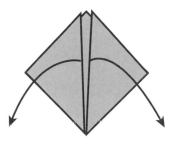

Bring the two corners back down and make a triangle again.

4

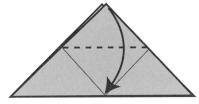

Fold down the top corner.

5

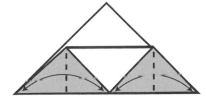

Fold the two bottom corners so that they meet. Unfold them again.

6

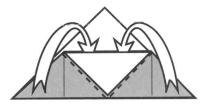

Fold the two triangles on the bottom left and right corners up and over the folded white triangle. Push the two corners inside the paper, behind the white triangle.

7

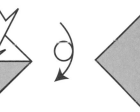 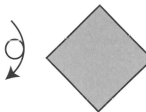

You have one of the world's greatest bookmarks! You can decorate the bookmark any way you like!

8

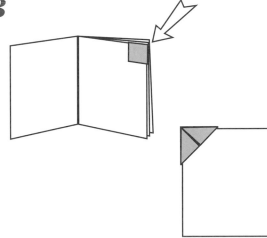

Place the bookmark in a page of this book. See how nicely this bookmark fits? Place the large square side of the bookmark on the page you are reading. If you open the book to the back side of the bookmark, you will know that you were not reading this page.

Heart

Everyone who learns how to make origami should know how to fold a heart. Unlike the other origami projects in this book, the heart uses one cut. Even though many origami designs do not use cutting today, traditional Japanese origami did use cuts. Only recently have origami designs **discouraged** cutting. This heart is simple and beautiful. You do not have to wait until Valentine's Day to use this origami. Leave an origami heart as a thank-you or give one to somebody that you love. Use any type of paper that you like, and fold to your heart's content.

1

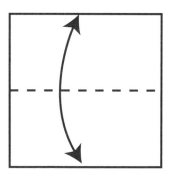

Begin with a square piece of paper of any size. If you are using origami paper, start with the white side up. Fold the paper in half and then unfold it. You should have a crease that divides your paper in half across the middle. Rotate the paper so that the crease line goes from the top to the bottom, or vertically.

2

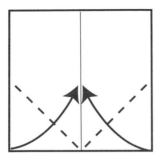

Fold the two bottom corners to the center line. The bottom of the paper will be pointed.

3

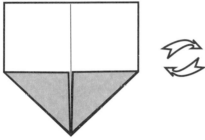

Rotate the paper so that it looks like a house with a colored roof.

4

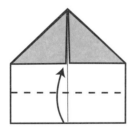

Fold the bottom edge of the house to the bottom edge of the colored roof.

5

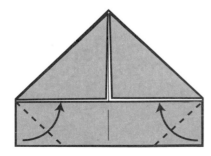

Fold up the two bottom corners so that their edges touch the bottom of the roof.

6

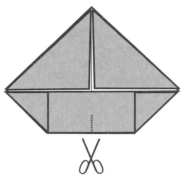

Using a pair of scissors, carefully cut from the middle of the bottom edge halfway up to the roof.

7

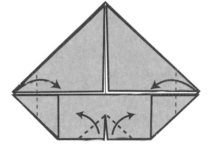

Follow the arrows in the design and fold in each of the four corners.

8

Turn it over and see the finished heart.

19

Fox Box

You will find many uses for this clever little box. It is a gift box, a puzzle, a bead, and a fortune cookie! Larger papers make larger boxes and tiny papers make tiny boxes. See how small a box you can make. The smallest ones can be strung like beads. Add a piece of candy and a note to a Fox Box and you have a paper fortune cookie! The folded papers look like three little fox heads, so this design is named the Fox Box.

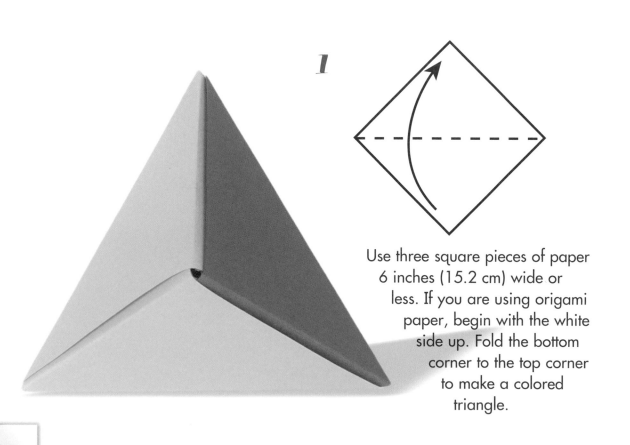

1

Use three square pieces of paper 6 inches (15.2 cm) wide or less. If you are using origami paper, begin with the white side up. Fold the bottom corner to the top corner to make a colored triangle.

2

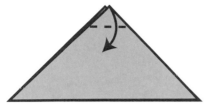

Fold down a small part of the top front corner. This will be the fox's nose.

3

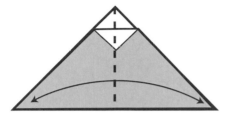

Fold the triangle in half. Then unfold.

4

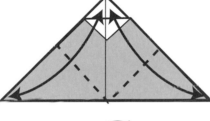

Fold the two bottom corners to the top square corner.

5

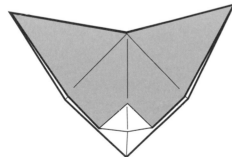

Unfold and rotate the paper so that the "nose" is at the bottom. Do you see the tall, pointy ears and the triangular face? Do you see how the fox's mouth opens under his nose? If you make three fox heads, you can build a Fox Box.

6

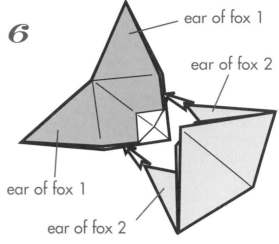

ear of fox 1

ear of fox 2

ear of fox 1

ear of fox 2

To make a Fox Box, just remember that "ears go into mouths." Each fox box will eat both ears of the other fox. Fit two foxes together by pushing both ears of fox #2 into the mouth of fox #1.

7

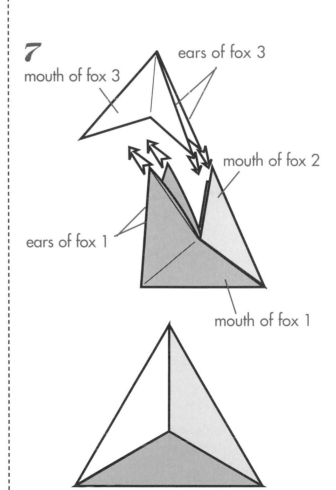

mouth of fox 3

ears of fox 3

mouth of fox 2

ears of fox 1

mouth of fox 1

Add fox #3 by pushing its ears into the mouth of fox #2.

Origami Key

1. MOUNTAIN FOLD

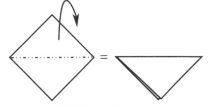

mountain fold line

To make a mountain fold, hold the paper so the white side is facing up. Fold the top corner back (away from you) to meet the bottom corner.

2. VALLEY FOLD

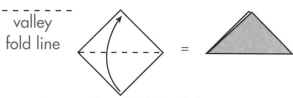

valley fold line

To make a valley fold, hold the paper so the white side is facing up. Fold the bottom corner up to meet the top corner.

3. TURN OVER

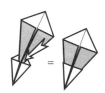

4. ROTATE

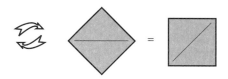

5. MOVE or PUSH

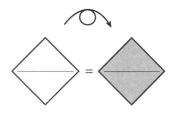

6. CUT

7. FOLD and UNFOLD

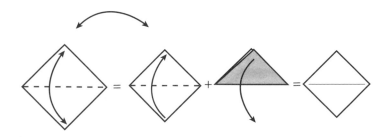

8. DIRECTION ARROW

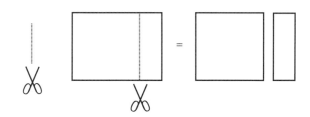

Glossary

brilliant (BRILL-yent) Very bright, like the sun or a sparkling gemstone.

create (kree-ATE) To build, make, or design something.

damaging (DA-mih-jing) To break, dent, ruin, or harm something.

discouraged (dis-KUR-ijd) To be advised against doing something.

invent (in-VENT) To create something new.

marks (MARKS) To hold a place. To show where something is by being next to it.

symbols (SIM-bulz) Objects or designs that stand for something else.

transformed (trans-FORMD) Changes its shape. Becomes something else.

Index

Web Sites

Due to the changing nature of Internet links, PowerKids Press has developed an online list of Web sites related to the subject of this book. This site is updated regularly. Please use this link to access the list:

www.powerkidslinks.com/kgo/maorsha/